Cambridge **Discovery Education**™

► **INTERACTIVE READERS**

Series editor: Bob Hastings

# ALTRUISM
## WHAT'S IN IT FOR ME?

W0099649

B1+

Brian Sargent

**CAMBRIDGE**
UNIVERSITY PRESS

◆**DISCOVERY**
EDUCATION™

CAMBRIDGE UNIVERSITY PRESS
Cambridge, New York, Melbourne, Madrid, Cape Town,
Singapore, São Paulo, Delhi, Mexico City

Cambridge University Press
32 Avenue of the Americas, New York, NY 10013-2473, USA

www.cambridge.org
Information on this title: www.cambridge.org/9781107622623

© Cambridge University Press 2014

This publication is in copyright. Subject to statutory exception and to the provisions
of relevant collective licensing agreements, no reproduction of any part may take place
without the written permission of Cambridge University Press.

First published 2014

Printed in Hong Kong, China, by Golden Cup Printing Company Limited

*A catalog record for this publication is available from the British Library.*

*Library of Congress Cataloging-in-Publication Data*

Sargent, Brian, 1969-
  Altruism : what's in it for me? / Brian Sargent.
     pages cm. -- (Cambridge discovery interactive readers)
  ISBN 978-1-107-62262-3 (pbk. : alk. paper)
  1. Altruism--Juvenile literature. 2. English language--Textbooks for foreign speakers.
  3. Readers (Elementary) I. Title.

BJ1474.S35 2013
171'.8--dc23

                              2013016509

ISBN  978-1-107-62262-3

Additional resources for this publication at www.cambridge.org

Cambridge University Press has no responsibility for the persistence or
accuracy of URLs for external or third-party Internet Web sites referred to in
this publication and does not guarantee that any content on such Web sites is,
or will remain, accurate or appropriate.

Layout services, art direction, book design, and photo research: Q2ABillSMITH GROUP
Editorial services: Hyphen S.A.
Audio production: CityVox, New York
Video production: Q2ABillSMITH GROUP

# Contents

# Before You Read: Get Ready!

Altruism means helping others. Whenever you do something good for someone else, you are being altruistic. It may seem a simple subject, but it is not. Many of the world's best thinkers have wondered about why people help others.

## Words to Know

stranger

researcher

donate

biology

**Match the highlighted word with its definition below.**

**1** I didn't know the person next to me on the bus. He was a stranger.

**2** The researcher interviewed 200 people for the study.

**3** Those clothes are too small for you now. You should donate them.

**4** My favorite subject is biology because I love animals.

**a** a person who studies a subject to learn information

**b** give something to someone who needs it

**c** a person you have never met before

**d** the study of living things

# Words to Know

**Read the paragraph and answer the questions.**

A scientist studied a group of children. He gave each child ten candies. He said they could eat them all or they could share them with someone. The scientist told the children that they would not get a reward either way. Most children chose to make a sacrifice and to share their candies with another child anyway.

**1** What is the meaning of "share" in the paragraph?

- **a** be part of a group
- **b** divide something between two or more people

**2** What is the meaning of "sacrifice" in the paragraph?

- **a** complaint
- **b** giving up something that is valuable to you

**3** What is the meaning of "reward" in the paragraph?

- **a** something given for good behavior
- **b** something bad or against the law

**Video Quest**

**Rescue**

Watch this video about three mountain climbers caught in a dangerous snow storm. What happened when one man couldn't help anymore?

# CHAPTER 1

# What is Altruism?

**PEOPLE HELP PEOPLE. WE SEE IT EVERY DAY. HAVE YOU EVER WONDERED WHY?**

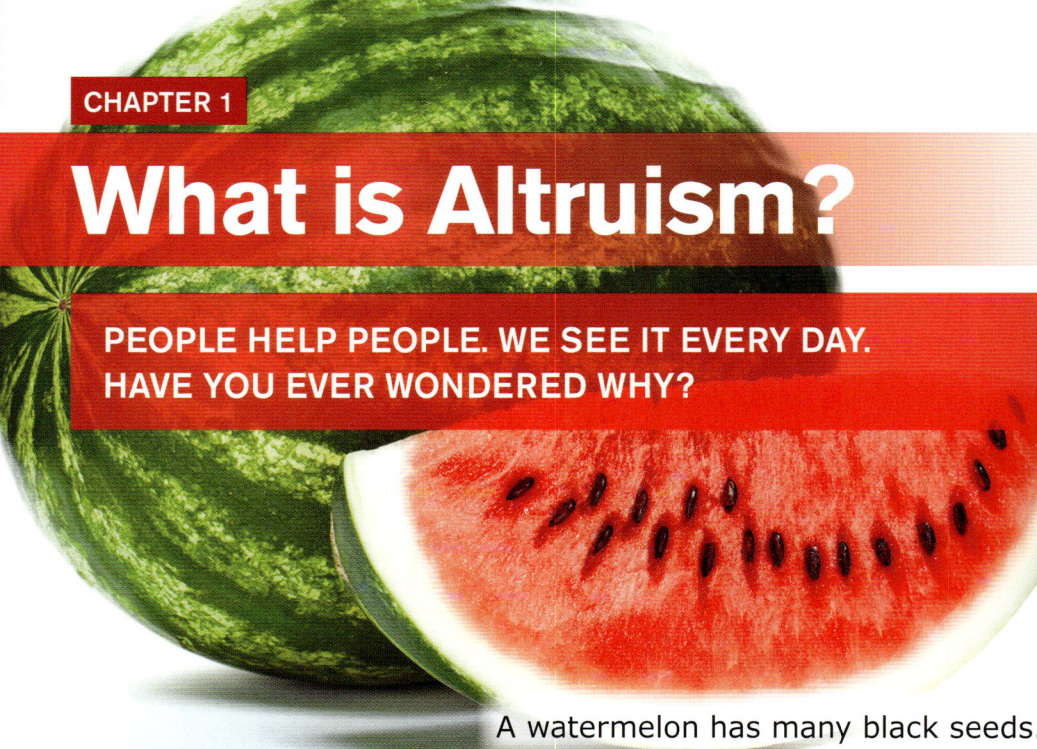

A watermelon has many black seeds.

There is an old Indonesian story about altruism. It is called "The Golden Watermelon."

Long ago, a rich man died. His two sons each received half of the man's money. The older son, Muzakir, took his money and locked it in a strong box. He didn't share it with anyone. The younger son, Dermawan, was kinder. Dermawan shared his money with people who had none.

Many people heard about Dermawan's kindness. They came to him and asked for money. Soon, Dermawan had no money left. Muzakir laughed at him and called him a fool.

One day, a bird with a broken wing fell into Dermawan's yard. Dermawan took care of the bird. He fed it rice from his own bowl. When the bird was better, it flew away. Later it returned and dropped a watermelon seed into Dermawan's garden. A watermelon grew, filled with pure gold!

Muzakir learned about the golden watermelon. He caught a bird and broke its wing. Then he kept the bird and gave it old, bad rice. When the bird was better, it flew away, and Muzakir waited for his watermelon seed.

Soon the bird returned with a seed. However, when Muzakir's watermelon grew, it was filled with disgusting, smelly dirt. The dirt covered Muzakir, and he ran away. Everyone laughed at him.

In this story, Dermawan does good things for others, but altruism is more than that. Altruism must include making a **sacrifice**. Dermawan made a sacrifice when he gave his money away, and when he gave the bird rice from his own bowl. Both times, Dermawan showed what it means to be altruistic.

**? ANALYZE**

Why did Muzakir catch a bird and break its wing? What was he feeling? What did he hope for?

# CHAPTER 2

# Learning to Be Good

**PARENTS SPEND A LOT OF TIME TEACHING THEIR CHILDREN TO SHARE, AND IT WORKS. SCIENTISTS FOUND IF YOU GIVE CHILDREN MONEY, THEY WILL PROBABLY SHARE IT, EVEN WITH STRANGERS!**

For years, scientists and researchers have wondered about altruism. Why are people altruistic? Why would people sacrifice themselves to help others? One idea is that **rewards** teach people to be altruistic.

The story of Muzakir and Dermawan is important. It is a teaching story for children. It teaches that altruism brings rewards. It also shows the bad results of being selfish. The story means to encourage young people to follow Dermawan's example – to be generous, selfless (not selfish), altruistic.

The story of "The Golden Watermelon" is not unusual. Many children's stories teach the same lesson. "Help others," the stories say, "and good things will happen to you."

In 2012, Brendan Haas, a 9-year-old American boy, earned a family trip to Disney World in Orlando, Florida, USA. He earned it by trading[1] on the Internet. He began with a toy soldier and offered to trade it for something a little nicer. Then he traded for something a little nicer again. Each trade became more valuable. After four months, Brendan finally had the Disney vacation.

However, Brendan didn't earn the trip for his own family. He earned it for a family he had never met. He gave the vacation to the family of a soldier who had died. Almost immediately, the boy became famous. His story appeared in many newspapers. He was interviewed on television. Then, because of his altruism, Disney World gave Brendan a trip for his own family.

Children are often happy to share money with others.

---

[1] **trade:** give something to someone else and get another thing back from them

Studying the human brain

It is easy to see how rewards such as this can encourage altruism. But some people say that altruism based on reward is not true altruism at all. If we give to others only because we hope to be rewarded, then we are actually being selfish. Does this explain Brendan's actions? It seems not. When he received the Disney World trip for his own family, he didn't accept it. Like the first trip, he gave it away to another family.

Brendan did not keep the second Disney World trip, but that does not mean he was not rewarded. Some scientists have discovered another reward for altruism: it feels good.

Recently, a group of researchers studied **charities**. A **charity** is an organization that gives money, food, or other help to people who need it. There are charities for many different needs, such as education, medical **research**, or to fight poverty.[2]

[2]**poverty:** when you are very poor

Many people around the world **donate** money and other things to charity because they want to help others. The researchers wanted to learn why people do this.

The researchers gave money to a group of people. Then they told the people they could keep the money or donate it to charity. While the people decided, the researchers studied their brains. The human brain has areas that become active[3] when the person feels happiness and love. Researchers found that donating money to charity made these places in the brain active. In other words, giving money away made the people feel happiness and love.

Why would giving money away create good feelings? Perhaps it is because we are taught to do so. We are told from childhood that giving is important. We are told that good people share what they have. So when we share, we feel happy. Our brains reward us for being good.

[3] **active:** excited, showing action

Parents and teachers have many ways to teach children to be altruistic. They can read stories of altruism to children. They can talk about examples of altruistic acts. They can even tell their children to play video games.

For many years, researchers have studied video games. Mostly, they have studied violent video games. Violent video games are games in which a player hurts or kills others in the game. The researchers wondered if violent video games create violent people. However, in 2009, some researchers decided to test the opposite idea. They wanted to know if video games could teach people to behave altruistically.

The researchers asked people to play special video games. In the games the player helps others. In one game, the player helps a family do housework. In another, the player cleans an island covered in pollution.

After the people were finished playing the video games, the researchers asked them to help a **stranger**. The stranger was trying to earn $10. The player could make it easy or difficult for the stranger to earn the money. After the people played helpful video games, they usually chose to make it easy for the stranger to earn the money.

The researchers also studied people playing violent video games. They found that those players often chose to make it difficult for the stranger to earn the money.

Research like this shows that altruism can be learned. We can train ourselves to help others. In addition, when we help others, we feel good about it. This is good news for teachers and parents who want to encourage altruism in children. But is there more to altruism?

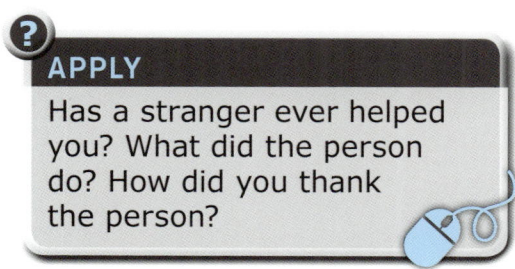

**?**

**APPLY**

Has a stranger ever helped you? What did the person do? How did you thank the person?

# CHAPTER 3

# The Biology of Altruism

**YOU ARE STANDING IN FRONT OF A BURNING BUILDING. YOU HEAR SOMEONE INSIDE. DO YOU HELP? DO YOU EVEN HAVE A CHOICE?**

On a cold January afternoon in New York City, Wesley Autrey and his two daughters were waiting for a subway train. Autrey was taking his daughters home before he went to work. Next to them, a 20-year-old man had a seizure[4] and fell down onto the subway tracks. Autrey immediately jumped down after him.

For a few moments, Autrey tried to lift the man off the tracks and onto the platform, but he could not do it. A train was coming. Quickly, Autrey lay down between the tracks on top of the young man. He covered the man's body with his own.

[4]**seizure:** a quick and unexpected illness or nervous attack

The train passed just centimeters above them – it hit Autrey's hat. But, both men were safe. After the subway train stopped, Autrey called out to his daughters and said he and the man were okay. Everyone on the subway platform clapped.

Wesley Autrey

Why did Wesley Autrey leave his daughters to jump down and help a stranger? When he could not lift the stranger to the platform, why did he stay and cover him, knowing they could both die?

Human history is full of similar stories.

- At 3 a.m. on an October morning in Maryland, 32-year-old Craig Cross ran into a burning building to save his neighbor, a man he hardly knew. Cross didn't even stop to put on his shoes first.

- In Louisiana, an 83-year-old woman accidentally drove into a lake. An 81-year-old woman, Carolyn Kelly, saved her, swimming almost twenty meters to the center of the lake. "Somebody had to do it," Kelly said, "and I was the only one who could."

Stories like these all involve people doing something very dangerous to help others. Scientists have an idea why they do it: it's biology.

Researchers often study animals to learn about people.

Biology is the study of living things. Biologists are often interested in altruism. They wonder why one living thing would sacrifice itself for another living thing. To find the answer, they sometimes study animals.

In 2011, a group of scientists led by Peggy Mason of the University of Chicago tested a group of rats. They put two rats together. One was free to move around. The other was trapped[5] in a small cage. Most times, the free rat was extremely unhappy because the other rat was trapped. But it didn't move away. It stayed close and kept biting the metal bars of the cage until it finally managed to open the cage and let the other rat out.

[5]**trapped:** unable to move or escape

Mason added chocolate to her study. She gave the free rat chocolate chips. Surprisingly, the free rat did not usually eat the chips right away. Instead, it opened the cage first, then it shared the chocolate with the other rat.

Like Mason's rats, studies show humans naturally want to help others. "Helping . . . is part of our biology," Mason says. For humans, however, getting help is sometimes complicated. If you need help, people may look at your skin color, age, or whether you are a man or a woman. Receiving help may even depend on your mood.[6] One study showed people are more likely to help you if you are smiling.

Two French researchers asked a person to walk around a supermarket. Half of the time, the person smiled at strangers. Half of the time, the person did not. Then the person dropped something, and the researchers counted how many strangers came to help. They learned that more strangers helped when they had seen the person smile first.

[6]**mood:** the way somebody feels

17

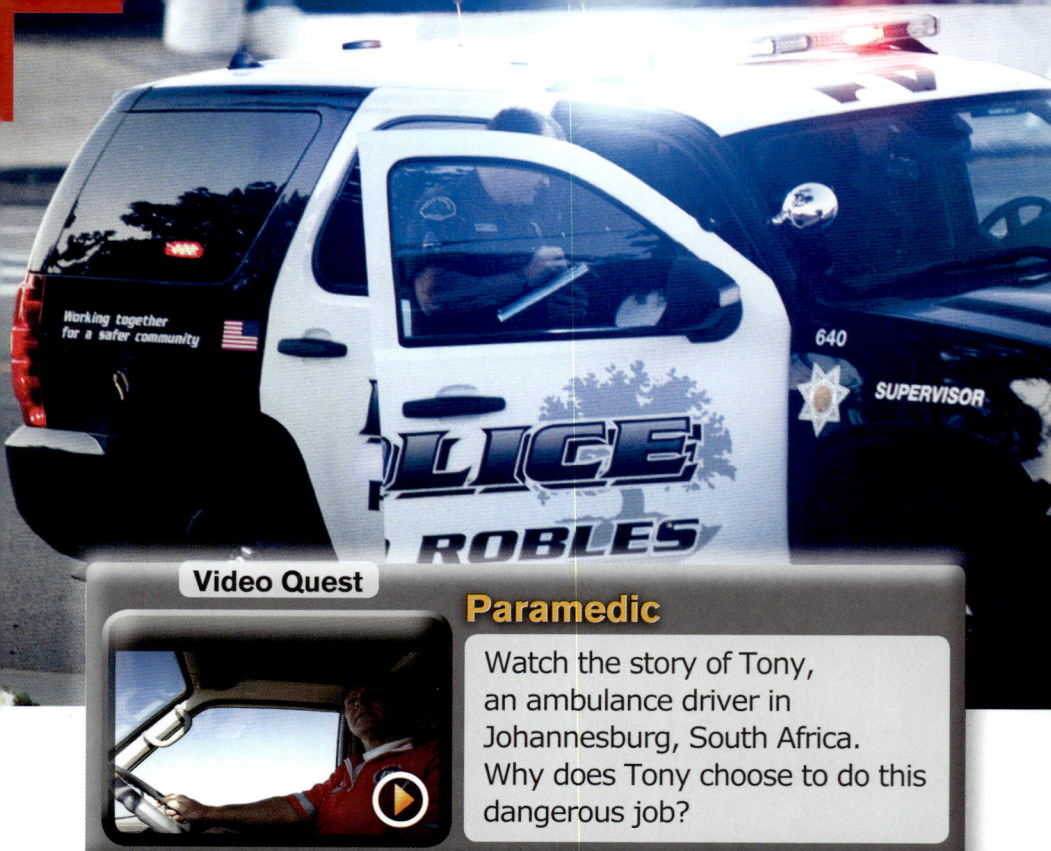

**Video Quest**

**Paramedic**

Watch the story of Tony, an ambulance driver in Johannesburg, South Africa. Why does Tony choose to do this dangerous job?

To see both the good and the very, very bad sides of human altruism, we can look at the terrible story of Hugo Alfredo Tale-Yax.

About 6 a.m. on a spring morning in 2010, a video camera recorded Tale-Yax being a hero. A woman was walking down a street in Queens, New York. A man followed her. He pulled out a knife and attacked her. Tale-Yax appeared and tried to stop the attacker. The woman was able to run away, but her attacker stabbed[7] Tale-Yax with the knife. Tale-Yax fell to the ground and did not move.

[7]**stab:** use something sharp and pointed, like a knife, to hurt someone

For the next hour, more than twenty people walked past Tale-Yax. Many looked at him, but kept walking. One stopped and lifted him up. He saw blood, and he turned and walked away. Two people stopped and took a picture of the dying man with their phones. Finally, just after 7 a.m., someone called the police but the caller gave the wrong address by mistake. Another call came at 7:21. The police came and found that Tale-Yax had died.

If people are naturally helpful, why did no one help Hugo Alfredo Tale-Yax? Perhaps they did not help because he appeared homeless.[8] Perhaps they did not help because they were frightened. Maybe they believed someone else had already called the police. Whatever the reason, Hugo Alfredo Tale-Yax died.

[8] **homeless:** without a place to live

# CHAPTER 4

# Why Do We Help Each Other?

**IS ALTRUISM SOMETHING WE LEARN? IS IT NATURAL? THE ANSWER TO BOTH QUESTIONS SEEMS TO BE "YES."**

In many cases, humans are naturally altruistic. In others, we choose altruism because we were taught to. The goal of altruism is helping. Perhaps we are helping to make ourselves feel better. Or perhaps we are helping others so they will help us back someday. For example, look at the vampire bat.

Many people have bad feelings about vampire bats. It is easy to see the reason. Vampire bats drink the blood of other animals, like cows or sheep. Sometimes they even drink the blood of people. Vampire bats must eat every day to stay healthy. If they miss two or three days, they die.

Missing days, however, is common for vampire bats. They are often not successful in finding blood. But instead of dying, they are helped by other bats in the group. Successful bats give hungry bats some of their own food. They bring it up from their stomach and share it through their mouth.

Biologists call this **reciprocal** altruism. That means sometimes a bat helps others, but other times it receives help instead. The group of bats stays alive because they make sacrifices for each other.

Many biologists believe that humans act the same way. They make sacrifices for each other. This allows the group to live and be successful.

Video Quest

## Meerkats

Watch this video about meerkats. What special way do they have of helping each other?

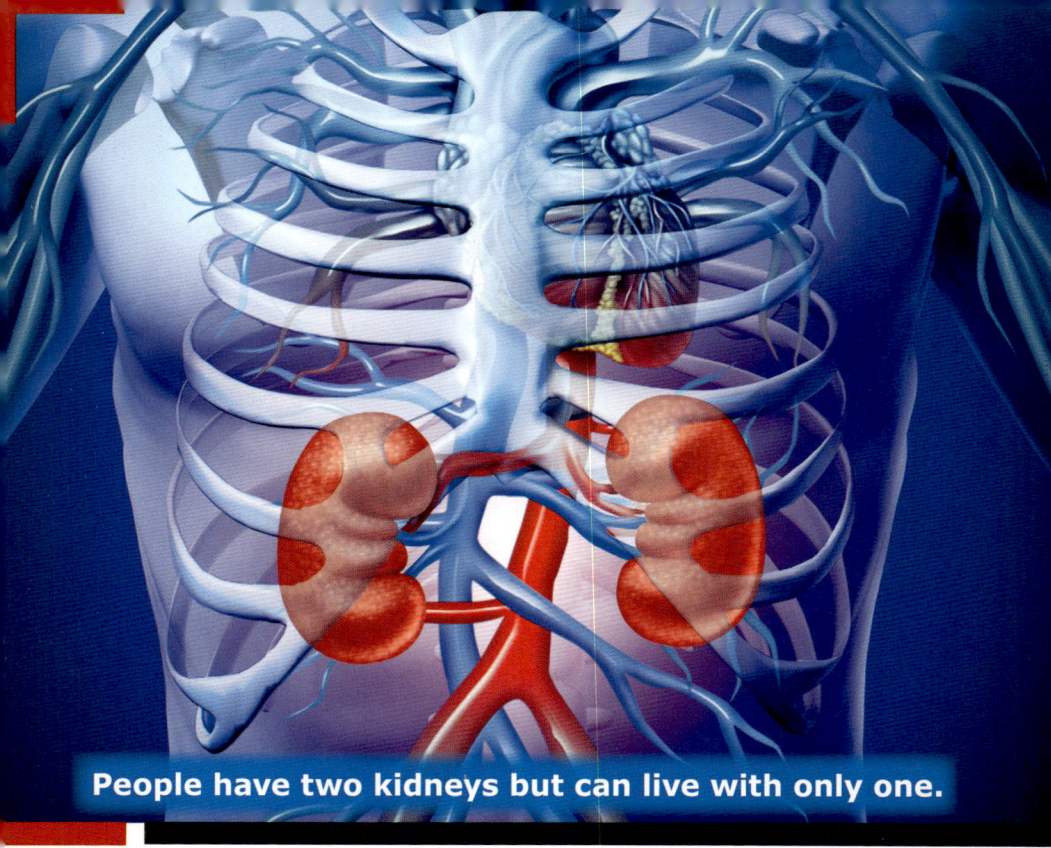

**People have two kidneys but can live with only one.**

In humans, reciprocal altruism can be very complicated. Feelings like friendship or dislike can change how people share. Also, people often judge how much sharing will cost them and how much they are likely to get back.

Vampire bats donate food to other vampire bats. People donate food to other people. This is easy to understand. Both vampire bats and people can always get more food. But what if a person donates something he or she can never get back? What if a person donates a part of his or her body to a stranger? That is exactly what 20-year-old Rachel Garneau did. Rachel donated one of her kidneys.[9]

.................................................................................................

[9]**kidney:** one of the two organs of the body that cleans our blood

People are born with two kidneys. If one fails, a person can still live, but if both fail, the person will die. However, kidneys can be transplanted. That means a healthy kidney can be taken from one person's body and put into another person's body. A kidney transplant is only successful if the new kidney matches the old kidney biologically. Kidney matching is very complicated and expensive, and matches are very difficult to find. Thousands of people die every year waiting for a match.

Rachel learned that her kidney matched a patient in New York City. She had never met the patient before, but she wanted to donate anyway. Kidney **donation** is not easy. Doctors had to do many tests on Rachel to make sure that she was healthy enough to donate and that her kidney was a perfect match. Then, they had to perform an operation[10] to take out the healthy kidney. Rachel had to stay in the hospital for several days after the operation.

[10] **operation:** when doctors cut a body open for a medical reason

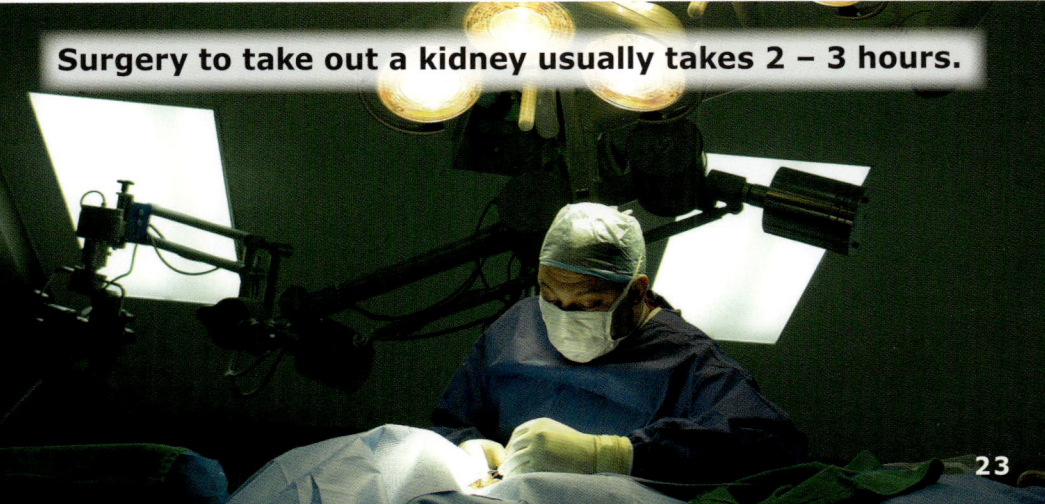

Surgery to take out a kidney usually takes 2 – 3 hours.

Rachel received no money for donating her kidney. She did it because she wanted to help someone. She did it for altruism.

Rachel's kidney donation began something amazing with the family of the patient who received Rachel's kidney. A member of the family had wanted to donate a kidney to the patient, but the kidney was not a match. Because Rachel donated her kidney to the patient – someone she didn't know – the family member donated a kidney to another person. Then a family member of that patient donated another kidney. That created more kidney donations.

Doctors call this a chain of altruistic donations. Sometimes chains can include many people. In 2011, a man in California began a chain that led to 30 kidney donations.

Donation chains are a type of altruism called "paying it forward." It is similar to but different from reciprocal altruism. In reciprocal altruism, you help someone because they will help you back. Paying it forward means you help someone and they don't help you back, but instead they help someone else. And then the next person helps someone else. And then that person helps someone else. It goes forward until someone chooses not to help.

It is hard to completely understand altruism, but it is easy to recognize it in the world around us. The word altruism means "living for others" or "selflessness." But many believe that altruism is not selfless at all. We always get something back when we give to others, even if it is only a feeling of pleasure.

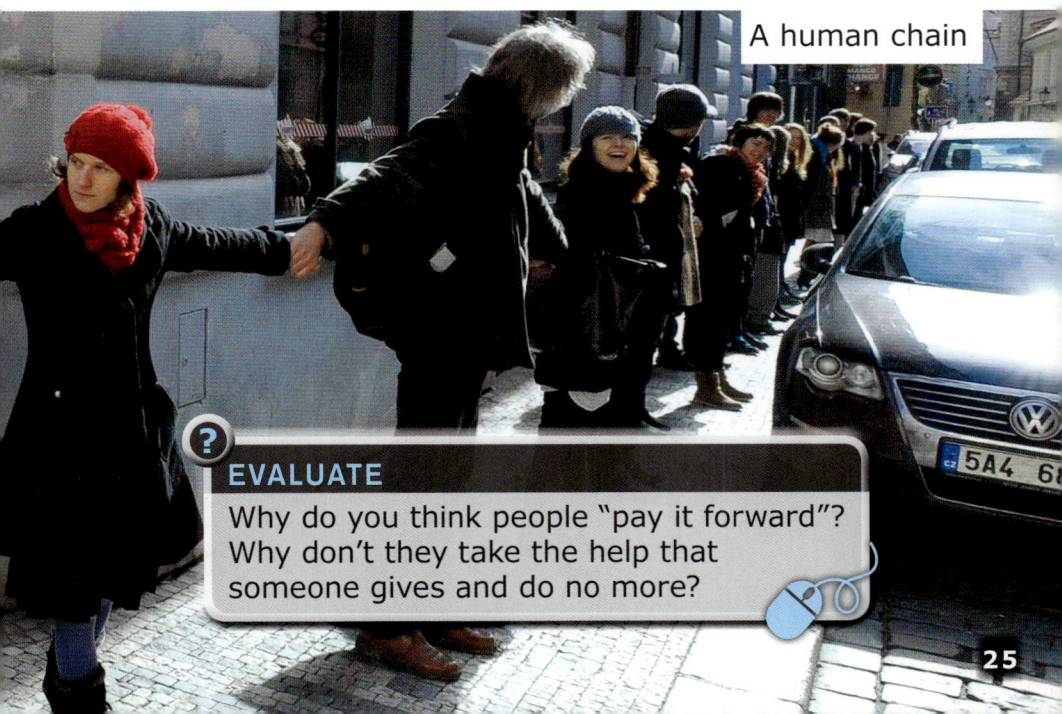

A human chain

**? EVALUATE**

Why do you think people "pay it forward"? Why don't they take the help that someone gives and do no more?

# CHAPTER 5

# What Would You Do?

**A LARGE PART OF ALTRUISM IS SHARING. RESEARCHERS INVENTED A GAME TO MEASURE[11] HOW PEOPLE SHARE.**

There is a game that researchers often use when studying altruism: the Dictator[12] Game:

- One person, the dictator, is given something valuable. Perhaps it is money or food. With children, it is often toys.

- The dictator can then choose to share with a stranger. The dictator does not know and will never meet the stranger.

The question is: Does the dictator share? If you were the dictator, would you share?

If you said "yes," you are like many others. In fact, about 80 percent of people choose to share in the Dictator Game. However, that is just the beginning.

How much do they share? Just a little? Half? Does it matter whether the "dictator" is a man or a woman?

[11] **measure:** discover the size or amount of something
[12] **dictator:** a leader who controls a country or people completely

Does it matter where the players are from? Ask yourself these questions. Do your answers surprise you?

Here is another type of Dictator Game:

- Like before, the dictator is given something valuable and can choose to share it with a stranger.

- This time, however, the stranger decides whether to accept it. If the stranger says "no," neither person gets anything.

For example: The dictator is given ten pieces of candy. He or she decides to share just one piece. The stranger, however, feels that one piece is unfair and refuses the offer. So, nobody gets any candy.

Imagine you are the stranger. How much do you expect? Should you be happy with anything or should you expect more? Research has found that most people expect at least 20 percent. Does this change what you feel about sharing?

# After You Read

Read the sentences and choose Ⓐ (True) or Ⓑ (False).

**1** Brendan Haas gave away the trip to Disney World to a friend.
   Ⓐ True
   Ⓑ False

**2** When people give money to charity, their brain activity remains normal.
   Ⓐ True
   Ⓑ False

**3** Wesley Autrey saved a stranger who fell onto subway tracks.
   Ⓐ True
   Ⓑ False

**4** Research shows rats never try to help each other.
   Ⓐ True
   Ⓑ False

**5** People are more likely to help someone if the person is smiling.
   Ⓐ True
   Ⓑ False

**6** Vampire bats show reciprocal altruism when they share food.
   Ⓐ True
   Ⓑ False

**7** Rachel Garneau received money and gifts for donating her kidney.
   Ⓐ True
   Ⓑ False

Video
**8** When the guard meerkat sounds the alarm, the other meerkats stop moving until the guard makes the "safe" sound.
   Ⓐ True
   Ⓑ False

## Complete the Sentences

Read the paragraphs and complete the sentences.

I was eating at my favorite restaurant. When I finished, the waiter told me a person had already paid for my meal. I asked what person, but the waiter could not show me. The person had already left. I looked around and pointed to someone I did not know. I took out my wallet and paid for that person's meal. Then I left.

**1** This story is an example of _____.

   (A) the Dictator Game

   (B) reciprocal altruism

   (C) paying it forward

When I was growing up, my mother worked two different jobs just so she could take care of me. She never had any time for herself. Because of her sacrifices, I always had enough to eat and new clothes to wear. When I got older, I went to a good university and earned my degree in business. Now I have a good job and am able to take care of my mother, just like she took care of me.

**2** This story is an example of _____.

   (A) paying it forward

   (B) reciprocal altruism

   (C) the Dictator Game

## Write

People who act altruistically are sometimes called heroes. Think of a story you know about a hero. Give a short version of the story and explain how the hero showed altruism in his or her actions.

_____

_____

_____

_____

_____

# Answer Key

**Words to Know, page 4**

**1** c **2** a **3** b **4** d

**Words to Know, page 5**

**1** b **2** b **3** a

**Video Quest, page 5**

The two other men left him to build a cave in the snow. Then they risked their own lives to return for him. They brought him to the cave they had built. All three survived.

**Analyze, page 7**

Muzakir was jealous of his brother's reward. He tried to repeat his brother's actions so that he would also get a golden watermelon.

**Apply, page 13**

*Answers will vary.*

**Video Quest, page 18**

Tony says that he does his job because that's just who he is, it's what he does. He wants to do it. He wants to help people.

**Video Quest, page 21**

One meerkat acts as a guard for the others. The guard gives a warning call if there is danger.

**Evaluate, page 25**

*Answers will vary.*

**True or False, page 28**

**1** B **2** B **3** A **4** B **5** A **6** A **7** B **8** B

**Complete the Sentences, page 29**

**1** C **2** B

**Write, page 29**

*Answers will vary.*